"I'm Proud of My Dad"

Written by
Hope Syndreamz

Illustrated by
Sky Owens

I'm Proud of My Dad
Published by Dumplinz Book Publishing
BRONX, NY 10467
(917) 642-5549
hopesyndreamz@optonline.net
www.dumplinzbookpublishing.com

ALL RIGHTS RESERVED

No part of this book may be reproduced or transmitted in any form or by any means—electronic or mechanical, including photocopying, recording or by any information storage and retrieval system without written permission from the authors, except for the inclusion of brief quotations in a review. Requests for permission or further information should be addressed to "The Permissions Department", hopesyndreamz@optonline.net

Dumplinz Books are available at special discounts for bulk purchases, sales promotions, fund raising or educational purposes. For details, contact: Special Sales Department, Dumplinz Book Publishing, (917) 642-5549 hopesyndreamz@optonline.net

Text Copyright © 2013 by Dumplinz Book Publishing
Illustrations Copyright © 2013 by Sky Owens
ISBN #: 978-0- 9964684-0-4
Library of Congress Control Number: 2015955154

Dedication

This book is dedicated to Carphetis "Peaches" Aiken; my partner in crime, as well as partner in laughter. You've looked after me, watched over me, and stood guard in spite of me for more than two decades now. So I say thank you…for all of the wonderful years achieved and yet to come.

This book is dedicated to my mother Juanita Wheeler, and in the wake of her absence…to all of my stand-in mothers:

Mom→ Marie Polite

Mom→ Shirley Madeline Owens

Mom→ Shirley Callaway

This book is dedicated to a young woman I consider the epitome of Momsà India Elieff, who has gone above and beyond the call of duty when it comes to her son Ryan who is Autistic and is loved, adored, cared for, and placed in the forefront in every aspect of her life.

My daddie's always working, and sometimes it might appear –

--when people come to our home, my daddie is never here.

But he is merely working, all day and night...night and day.
So when he comes home to us; he goes to bed right away.

I used to get upset and wish my daddie would stay home
But he has got to go to work; so I play home alone.

Lots of vital stuff to do; I get it, I understand.
That's what it means to be adult; a dad….to be a man.
I get to see him every Sunday, before I go to sleep.
He comes in; reads me a book; together we count sheep.

I don't know what my daddie does, all I know is…it's real big.
I imagine he's a trucker, with a huge red and gold rig.

When he comes home dirty; I imagine he's found a fossil.
With all the dirt he's bringing home, that bone must be colossal.

When he comes in soaking wet,

I see a deep sea diver

And when he pulls out all his tools,
I think he's a MacGyver.

I really don't know
what he does for a living;
I ask every chance I get.
But his reply just skips by,
and he quickly changes
the subject.

I hear them talking. Mommie says,
"*Hunnii, just tell Amir.
He wants to know so badly
of his father's great career.*"

But daddie shakes his head
at her and says,
"NO, LOVE…IT'S WAY TOO SOON.
I PROMISE TO TELL AMIR ONE DAY."
Then he walks out of the room.

I go to sleep with wild ideas of what my daddie does.
Maybe when he retires he will tell me what he was.

I go to sleep
and while I dream,
I see him taming lions.

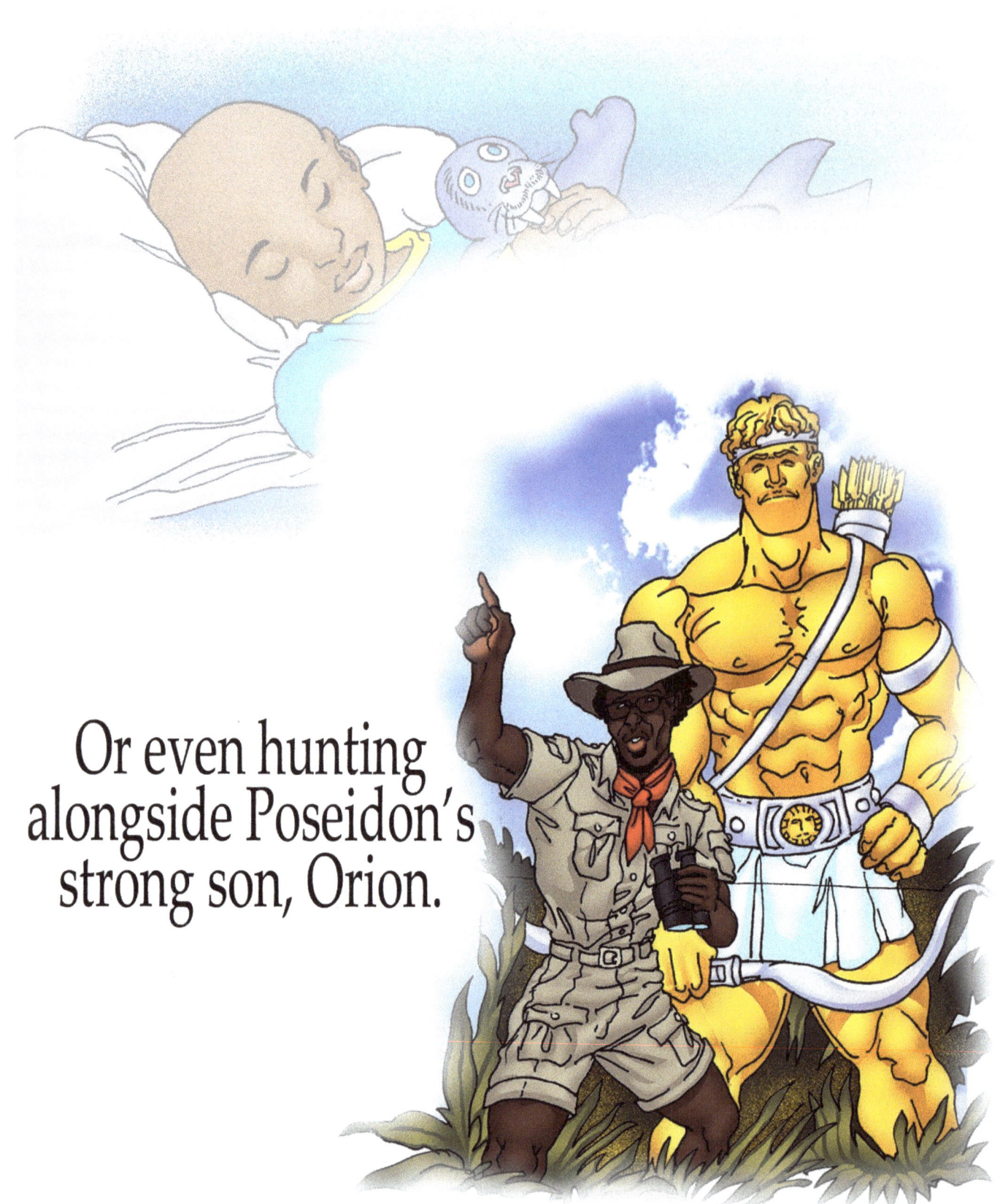

Or even hunting alongside Poseidon's strong son, Orion.

I dream he's climbing mountains, searching for the rarest herbs.

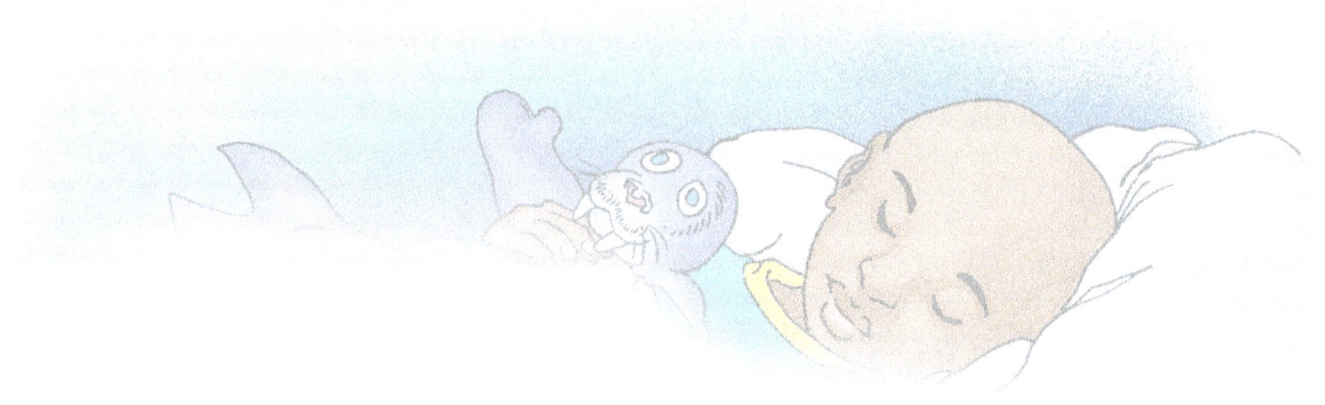

Possibly driving racing cars; sharp turns on hairpin curves.

I dream he's on the ocean searching for the deadliest catch.

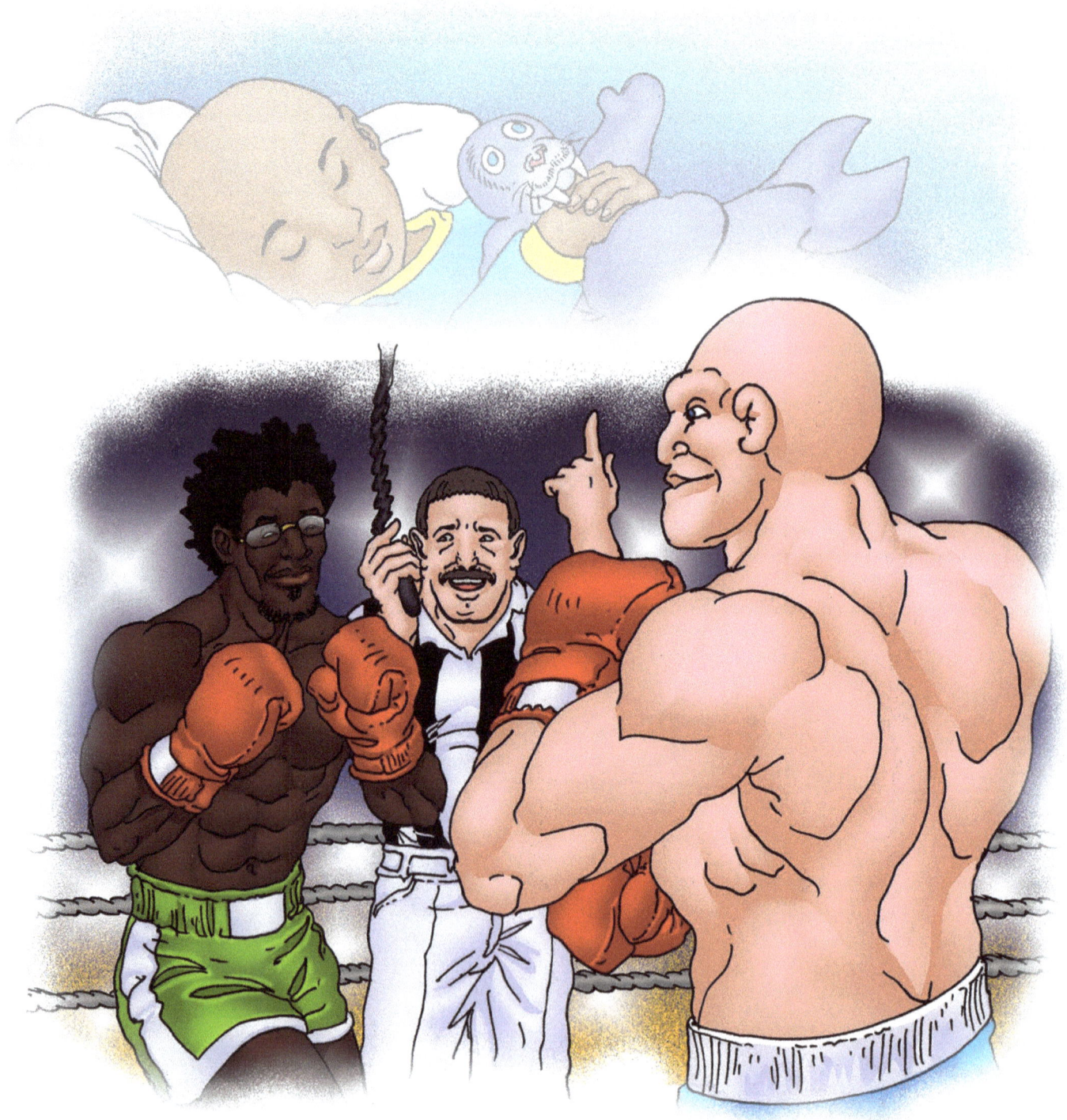

Or even in a large roped ring, fighting in a boxing match.

I dream he's crawling on his belly trying to catch a thief.

Or on a Native reservation;
maybe he's even the chief.

I turn back to the wall,
and erase all my thoughts for the night.
I've gotta get up early; school starts soon....
so I'll say goodnight.

The morning comes quick,
I'm spit shined and dressed for school; can't be late.
Today we find out
the topic for show and tell; I can't wait!!

The teacher hands out
a letter for us
to take home
for our parents to sign.

I read the notice quickly;
Yes! It's time for "Career Day!"
This is going to work out
juuuuust fine.

I'll finally find out what daddie does, all day when he's not at home.

Dad? Dad? Dad? Dad? Dad? Dad?

And this time he can't escape my words, run away, or jump on the phone.

Mommie came to my school last time.
I could still hear my class cheer.

The girls were proud to hear
she is an electrical engineer.

But my daddie always finds a way
to wiggle out of it.
He won't get away from me this time;
I'll just tighten my grip.

I asked my daddie if he'd come this time,
and I did not back down.
He said of course he would be there.
He doesn't want to see me frown.

So today's the day I get to learn
what daddie does for a living.
Jumped in his car, we sped off to school.
I couldn't stop my grinning.

We waited for all the other kids.
Their parents took their turn.
Lots of super careers in here.
So much information to learn.

Nadeem's dad is a carpenter.
He makes luxurious shelves.

Now...Zora's mother is a vet; she makes sure our pets stay well.

Hachiro's mother is a chef; she owns a small chain of restaurants.

David's dad owns a candy store, *treating us to whatever we want.*

Royboy's mom is a busy housewife.

But always makes time to chaperone our trips.

Mark's mom owns a franchise that makes world famous salsa dips.

I hold my breath as dad gets up;
walks up to the front of the class.
This is it, my friends; I'll finally learn
what daddie does at last.

He clears his throat,
takes off his coat,
and sits down in the chair.
He looks out into
the crowd of shining
faces with loving care.

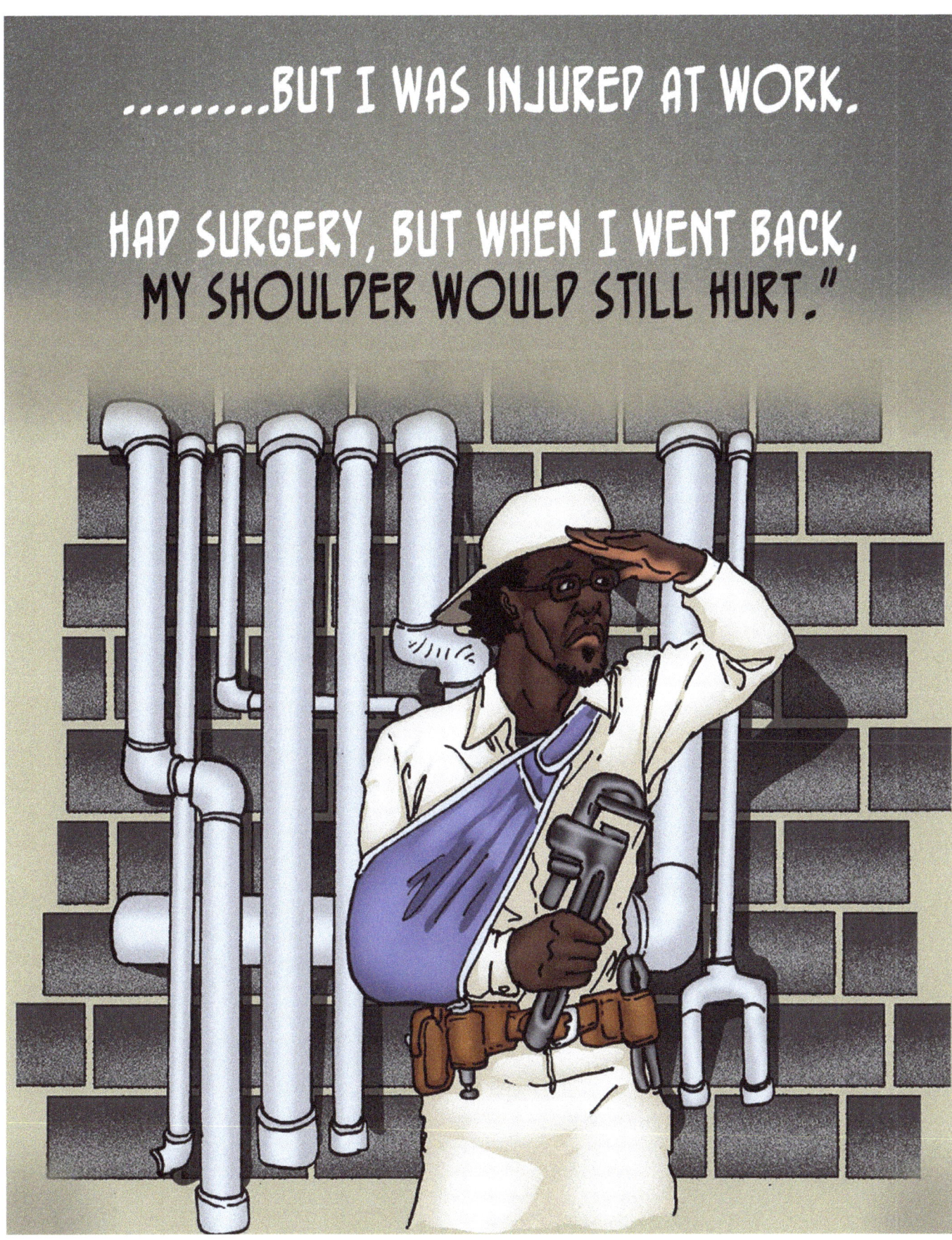

"SO I LEFT MY JOB, AND HIT THE STREETS IN SEARCH OF A NEW CAREER.
I TRIED A LOT OF DIFFERENT THINGS, BUT NONE THAT I HELD DEAR.

UNTIL I STARTED WORKING AS A SANITATION MAN.
YUP, I'M THE SMELLY GUY PASSING BY DRAGGING YOUR TRASH CANS."

I'D EMPTY THEM, RECYCLED GOODS TOO,
AND RETURN YOUR CANS BACK NICE.
I'D STOP BY TUESDAY AND SATURDAY,
AND SOMETIMES I'D COME BY TWICE."

When school was done we had fun;
my daddie, the others, and me.

They took us out for chips and dip,
and soda and it was free.

The other parents had to go but daddie took off the whole day

We piled in our car he drove us far, to a big park where we played.

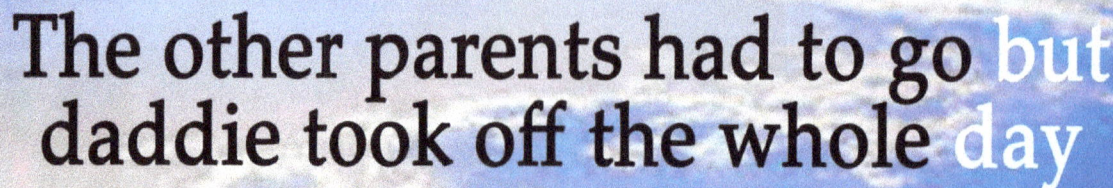

We laughed and laughed and played some more, and then the sun grew dim. Dad drove them home; everyone, and then it was just me and him.

We called mom's phone;
she wasn't yet home,
ran into her at the store.

She said, *"How about
we all eat out?"*
So they bought pizza and more.

We ate all the pizzas,
and drank our juices,
sodas, coffees too.

I got in mom's side
dad jumped in his ride,
mom said, *"Hunnii,
I'll follow you."*

I loved the day I spent with dad and mommie near the end. I loved how daddie took us out; me and all my little friends.

When we got home I ran upstairs;
undressed and washed up right.
So they wouldn't have to remind
me of my routine tonight.

Put on my jammies, said my prayers,
then mom read me a book.
But only half way; big day tomorrow...
and mommie has lots to cook.

I lie there thinking about my daddie, and the job he has.

He used to be a plumber's foreman... now he picks up trash.

They taught me not to judge a sole, no matter who they are.

So, I would never laugh or taunt. I'd treat them like a star.

They taught me sharing is crucial in life, no matter what the object.
They taught me not to put folks down, no matter what the topic.
They taught me smile at everyone, even strangers need love too.
They taught me never steal or disrespect; that will never do.

It's very wrong to joke about something someone cannot change.

We wouldn't want them to feel embarrassed, different or strange.

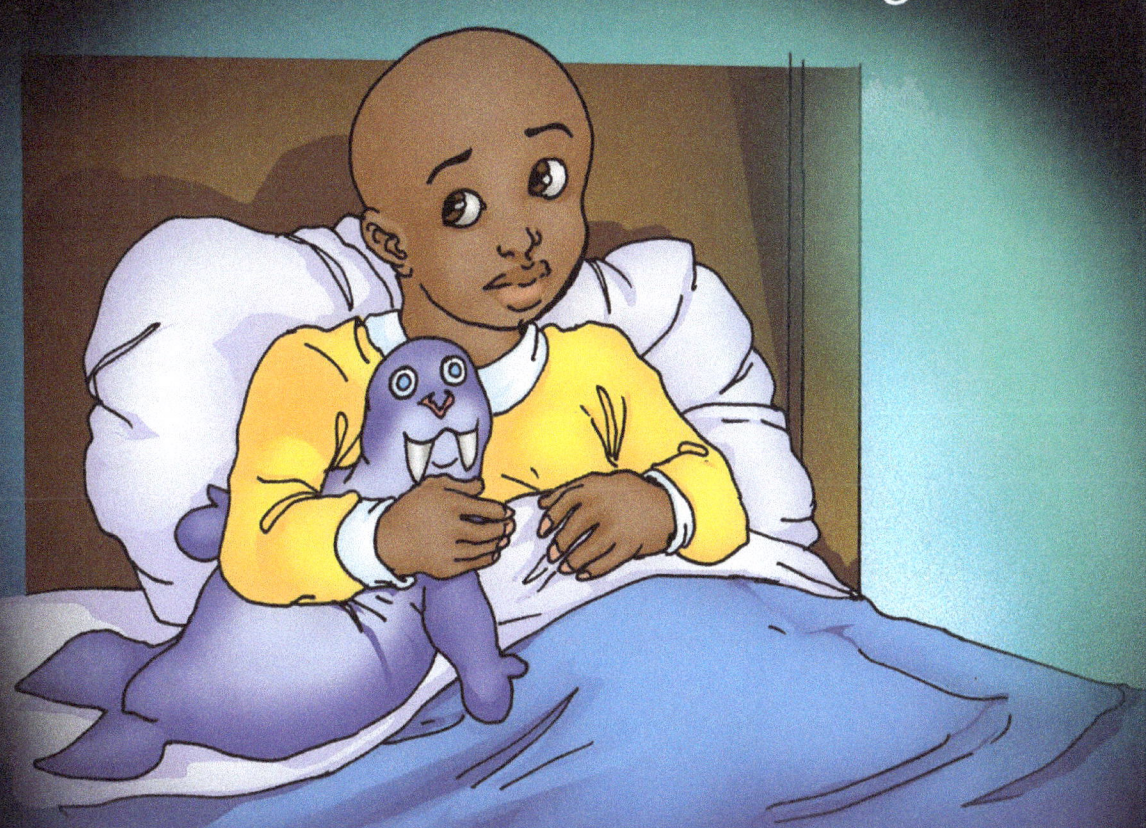

Everyone has a right to be happy, that's true no matter who they are. Bald, short, tall, thin, thick, hairy, full lips, braces or even a scar.

They taught me care for everyone,
no matter what their race.
This earth is big enough for all…
move over; make some space.

They taught me work is not an option,
everyone must do it.
And if you have a family,
you will have to just hop to it.

I learned that no one lives for free,
and working is a must.

The other parents taught me too;
to work without a fuss.

I see my daddie differently;
now that I understand.

It isn't easy growing up;
even harder to be a man.

I understand; when you're a dad...
your pride must take a back seat.

Your family needs a place to live,
and food that they can eat.

Daddie's pride is working not lounging around our home. So now I fully understand why I play alone.

And that's ok because today
I learned that he's like me.

He does a lot of different things
and likes to keep busy.

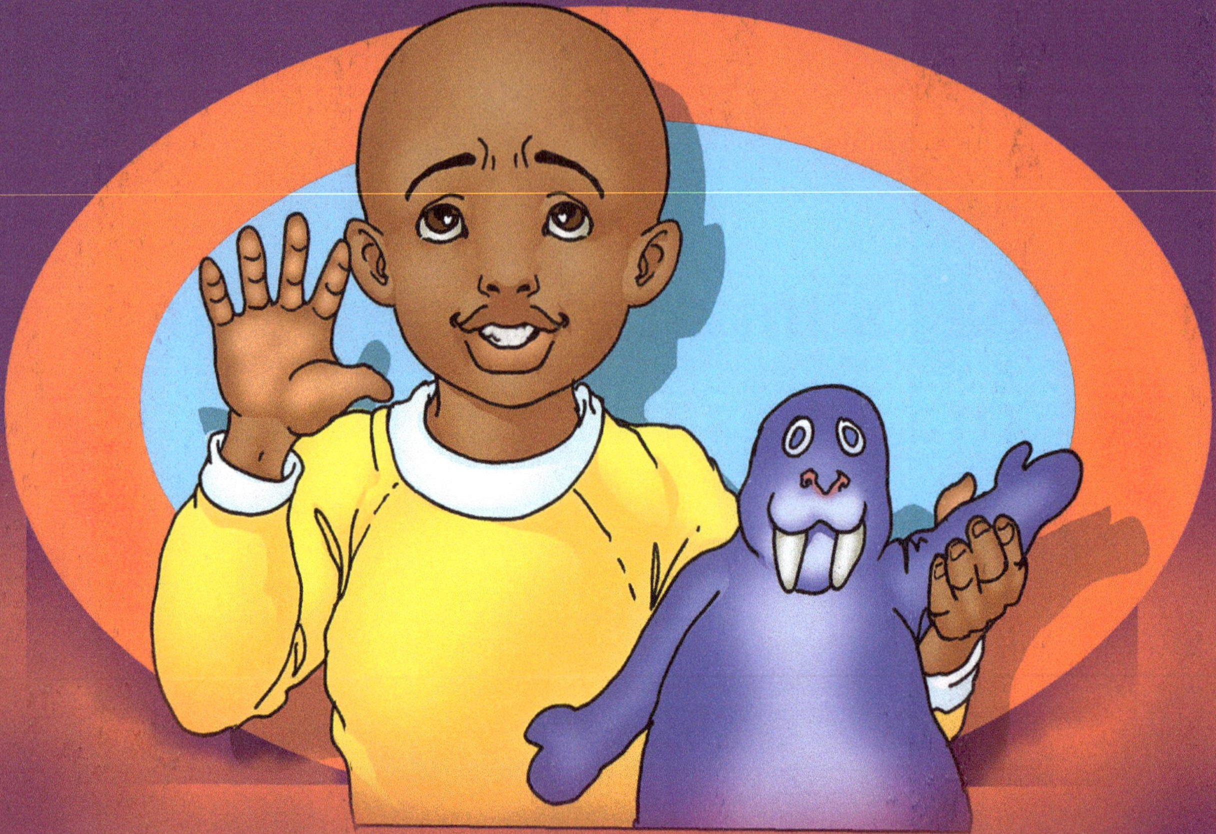

The day has gone and daddie's tucked me in for a long night's rest. I liked the other parents' jobs, but daddie's job is the best.

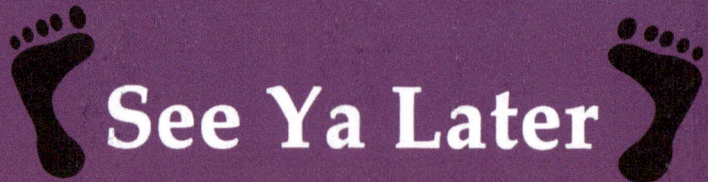

Acknowledgments

Well...I can now say...I finally did it. To be more specific...We did it. My first book, "I Love My Hoodie" was a success. A small success...but a success, nevertheless, and climbing. I couldn't be any more proud of it than I am right now. All praise belonging to my God in heaven, Jehovah for first granting me the ability to crank out such pretty words, and for giving me the courage, through his son Jesus Christ, to forge ahead and finish it.

I thank my artist/brother/little engine, Sky Owens for making all these great artistic flares possible. Had it not been for his colorful eye; none of my visions would have drawn breath and come to life on paper before our very eyes. Thank you for making my eyes yours, Sky...love you big bruhman.

I thank John Blasingame for believing in my talents enough to send me to his very dear and close friends Mr. & Mrs. Rose of Amber Communications Group, Inc. - http://www.lindennewday.com/frame.htm

I want to thank "ACGI" - Amber Communications Group Inc., for having faith in me enough to assist in making my Hope Syndreamz a reality. I love you Mr. & Mrs. Rose for believing in my story enough to help me print it. - http://amberbooks.com/

I want to thank my dear brother/Actor/Director/Producer/Published Author-Darryl Lacy, winner of the 2013 NAACP Image Award for Outstanding Literary Work – Debut Author, for his scripted work: "Nikki G: A Portrait of Nikki Giovanni in Her Own Words. I love you bruhman. - http://www.darryllacyproductions.com/

I thank everyone who attended my first ever launch party, Thank you Alabama Dots for catering my event. Thank you Debra and Holly for supporting me via two cases of wine expressly delivered to my door for said event. I love you ladies. - http://www.eventsful.com/.

Thank you Joann, for allowing me to have my very first book signing at one of your world famous establishments, "Make My Cake". - http://www.makemycake.com/.

Thank you, Sergio D, for interviewing me on your online radio show...Classicsoul 1075. - http://classicsoul1075.com/ and Ken Murph of the same online station, for interviewing me on your Manhattan cable television show, "Whatz Going On". I also want to thank his son who I affectionately refer to as "Little Kennii" for being the photographer for that event, as well as many more events to come.

I thank my best friend and partner in crime, Peaches for sticking it out with me, through all the launch parties, the book signings, and the networking she did on my behalf as well as in my absence.

Thank You

...Roy and Nadeem, our brothers from New Mexico for their support and constant uplifting and encouraging words. I thank my sister Idella J, and my online friend Lisa M for being the first people ever to purchase my book. Thank you Fred for always being ever vigilant, dependable, and punctual in carting me all over the place in order to independently sell my book. - http://www.ojandcompanylimo.com/

Thank you...

...one and all who've purchased my first book. This paragraph is especially for you. Your faith in my talents, your faith in my words, and your faith in my vision is what made "I Love My Hoodie" such a success.

This second installment of my Septology Saga, "I'm Proud of my Dad", was written a little differently. I felt this story deserved a deeper message, as it is actually intended for the parents and not for the children...per say. This story has a subliminal message to all parents who keep their children in the dark as to what it is they do for a living. I know of several parents who refuse to tell their children what it is that they do for a living. Be it because they feel it's actually of no consequence if they know, or because they're ashamed of what they do, even though it's being done to keep food on the table and keep a roof over their heads.

A job, to many an adult, is just that...a job, and think nothing more of it than to make ends meet, legally or otherwise. But what they don't or even fail to realize is that the mind of a mild, the world of a child is much smaller than theirs, and the knowledge that is shared makes a large impact on a little one who is constantly looking up at their parents for guidance and direction.

To a child...being a part of the family means more than just the occasional allowance, or presents, or even great report cards. Every child desires to be a part of the bigger picture. A little bit of adulthood throwing them a virtual bone. I used to want to know what my father did for a living, and he wouldn't tell me or explain it to me. It left me wondering and imagining all sorts of career choices for him. I would watch him leave the house very early in the morning and drive away.

I had no idea where he was going. All I knew was that he was going..."To Work". My mind was running wild trying to figure out what he did for a living. I knew mommie was a nurse. She told us stories, and taught us different aspects of her job on a constant basis. I guess that's why I know a little bit about medicine, and how the body works. Thanks mommie. Oh wait...that's also why I'm so OCD about washing hands for a long period of time, and what to do when water goes down your windpipe...thanks a lot mommie.

Anyway...It wasn't until I was a teenager that I learned of his job. But once I learned of his actual choice, I was thrilled, and very proud of him. He was an electrician, installing safes for banks. He worked for Diebold, in Lodi, New Jersey. And as I grew...I was given the opportunity to follow in his footsteps as an electrician for Amtrak. And it was because of that experience, I wrote this story. I hope you enjoy it as well.

May all of your Hopes N' Dreamz Come True

Hope Syndreamz

About The Team

AUTHOR: ISREBA WHEELER aka HOPE SYNDREAMZ has loved writing ever since she was in elementary school. At that time she was into poetry, and won a few poetry contests in school. Soon after, Isreba began to write stories for all of the children to read. The teachers told Isreba that her writing was over the heads of her classmates and when she got older, maybe then she should pursue writing as a career, but not now. So Isreba stopped writing...until she was an adult. Isreba joined a magazine staff for a while, but shortly thereafter connected with Illustrator Sky Owens and created Dumplinz Books.

Whenever Isreba is asked what inspired her to write children's books, she states, "Entertaining the vulnerable tiny fresh minds of our children today. Too much of life's negativity and nonsense trickles down into their bowls of cereal and they are forced to eat it up along with life's innocent lessons. I wanted to bring some morals and fun back into the eyes of these children, our children. I wanted to open up their mind's eye again, and help them recapture the essence of imagination." Isreba added, "I hope one day my children's books will inspire a child to sit me down when I am old and grey...make up a story off of the top of their heads, and tell me a story."

Isreba currently resides and works in Bronx, New York.

ILLUSTRATOR: PRESTON SKYLAR OWENS aka SKY OWENS first put crayon to paper at the tender age of 3, inspired by his mother and greatest fan. An avid fan of cartoons and comic books, he followed his passion for all of his life, working for such companies of Marvel, DC, and Dark Horse as a ghost artist, until he caught his first break as a solo artist with Fantagraphic comix, Antarctic Press, Lost Cause Production, London Night Studios until he finally self-published under Box Press and finally Action Bunny Comix. Self-taught from the beginning, he now uses the classic art methods of pencil, pen & ink, furthering his abilities with computer augmentations, bringing a new life to his illustrations. He now works and resides in a small town in New Jersey, enjoying his craft, bringing many creators' ideas to light.

www.ingramcontent.com/pod-product-compliance
Lightning Source LLC
Chambersburg PA
CBHW061930290426
44113CB00024B/2867